The Karmic Curve

How to have it (nearly) all, but not all at the same time

by

Mary I. William*

For

PJBJK(?)A

Vincent Lustygier

Emmanuelle Hayward

Authors' note

Mary* and William* are a professional couple based in Brussels. They have three young children.

Mary* worked until recently in a large private sector organisation. She is currently taking a career break. She wrote this book with William*, who works in a large public sector organisation.

Between them they have around forty years of corporate and government experience.

Everything described in the book is based on their professional experience and life together.

But where a word is marked with an asterisk (*), it has been changed in order to ensure total respect for confidentiality.

Finally, having lived through some difficult times in recent years, Mary* and William* will donate 50 pence/ cents for every copy of this book sold via Amazon to http://www.actionforhappiness.org/.

"Action for Happiness" is a charity that aims to help anyone and everyone to be just that little bit happier, irrespective of the challenges they may be facing in life.

Prologue

Scott Fitzgerald's definition of an artist was someone who is capable of holding two conflicting positions at the same time, whilst continuing to function effectively.

Over the past decade, we have had lots of fun, got married, had lots more fun, had two great careers, had a daughter, had twin boys, and felt very deeply privileged, extremely lucky, and blessed.

Then we had an *annus horribilis.*

The death of William's* father was both sudden and tragic. The career side of things became comical bordering on farce. The kids were all essentially fine throughout, but winters in Brussels can be long, cold and dark, and when you have a 3-year-old and two 1-year-olds and everyone is ill all at the same time, and when both of you are really supposed to be in parallel meetings in two separate countries (neither of them the one in which you live) then something has to give. It did.

We both like to think that we have an artistic side, but even invoking Scott Fitzgerald proved to be woefully insufficient as it turned out. Enough *Schadenfreude* (for now), however. This book is not about what happened, but what we think we have learned along the way.

Because whilst many, if not most, people in the world have much more serious things to worry about on a daily basis (and we know that we are very lucky indeed), we are pretty sure that we are not the only household on the planet that is trying to juggle family responsibilities, corporate realities and the wish not to forget how to have fun.

So this is mainly a book about corporate leadership and its discontents, but <u>not</u> because we hold any grudge against either of our employers. We don't. Really. Both organisations were <u>outstanding</u> in the circumstances when things got tough.

But because in life, sadly, grandparents die, children get ill and parents get exhausted, or at least very tired. And they always will. These are immutable facts of life in times past, time present and time future. We might wish we could change them, but we can't.

The way that the world of work is organised, on the other hand, and the "narratives" that people live out - and maybe even, just occasionally, cling to - about "success", "leadership", "effectiveness" and all the rest *can* be changed. At least in theory.

We don't claim to know all, or quite possibly any, of the solutions, but this book is the sort of manual that might help you to apply the karmic brakes slightly earlier than we did. We hope, more than anything, that you enjoy it.

Introduction

Modern corporate and political life is harsh. Few people like to admit it, but it's true. The signs are everywhere, from Barack Obama's grey hairs to David Cameron's bald spot.

The ultimate reason for this is the seemingly limitless human capacity for envy. While we may admire great leaders from Winston Churchill to Steve Jobs, we all know in our hearts that they had to climb greasy poles and deal on a daily basis with the seething resentment of their peers before ascending to the peak of invincibility in their respective fields, at least for as long as it lasted.

Now there exist a few people for whom this is nothing but an unalloyed delight. It may just be the case that Donald Trump, whatever his follicle situation, genuinely thrives on inculcating fear in others and worries not one iota about the grievances and antipathy that he creates along the way.

But most of us are not like this. And wisely so. For whilst talented people always will and indeed should strive to rise up the pecking order in organisations, few of them will have failed to notice the strains that corporate and political leadership places upon those at the pinnacle. Or to put it another way, why is it that in Game of Thrones the advisors generally seem to outlive the rulers?

Bookshops and Kindle stores are full of treatises on corporate leadership, both how to attain it and how to practice it once obtained. We humbly recommend these titles to aspiring Donald Trumps.

This book attempts something more subtle: to put on paper the sum total of more than forty years of corporate and government experience in the interests of assisting those who wish to be citizens as well as corporate citizens. That is to say, to have a career but also to have time for a life beyond.

Not by doing anything radical. You can keep the iPhone and video conference to your heart's content. You might want to think twice, however, about getting a reputation for always replying immediately to your bosses, or for delivering quantity rather than quality.

The early 21st century is dripping with information. Most of us are constantly drowning in it. Anyone seeking to exert domination or total control over the flows of data that represent our modern corporate lives will ultimately fail. But it is fun watching The Donald try, and we wouldn't want to you miss out on that either.

If, however, you aspire to getting the best out of both your career <u>and</u> your life, then this book is here to help you give it a try – and hey, even if it doesn't work out, pretty much the worst that can happen is that you'll smile a bit more often whilst staring at your screen.

How the book is organised

Charlie Parker, the great jazz saxophonist, was once asked how he could play with such virtuoso improvisation. His reply: "First you have to learn the rules, then you have to learn how to forget them".

Well, life doesn't get much better than listening to Charlie Parker, so we are going to try to follow his advice. The book is therefore divided into four musically-themed sections.

The first section, "A Prelude to Karma" introduces the main ideas and concepts that we develop later in the book.

The second section, "Classicial Karma" gives you the techniques that we hope can help you to find a better balance between work, life and changing nappies (or similar).

The third section, "Jungle Boogie" goes off-piste and outside of the office to tackle those all-important coffees, lunches, cocktail receptions and – if you can stomach them – dinner parties.

And the final section, "Futuristic Karmic Jazz" tells you how we think things could become just that little bit more karmic in the future.

Perhaps.

A Prelude to Karma

1. Cracking ego (in secret)

All politics is local and so it is with corporate life. If you want to enjoy the privileges that come with insightful corporate living, you'll need to do a bit of work on yourself. This means getting to grips with your ambition. Not killing or choking it, just managing it.

Bosses hate this for one simple reason. The nakedly ambitious are among the easiest of office types to manipulate, by which read get to do more work for the same recompense. The core of this is <u>pride</u> – a recurrent theme of this book.

Our favourite example is "young man syndrome" or – for those with younger children and/ or longer memories – "Scrappy-Doo syndrome". If you need a reminder, Scrappy-Doo, nephew of the more insouciant Scooby, was the cartoon dog with the catch-phrase "Let me at 'em Uncle Scoob" whenever he was confronted with injustice or wrong-doing.

His enthusiasm wasn't the issue, nor indeed were his undoubted crime-fighting skills. The problem was that he had to have them permanently on display in the hope of getting a pat on the head. Psychoanalytically, it is perhaps not surprising that

Scrappy's father seems not to have been around for much of his life. But that is for another book.

Back in the real world, we know many outwardly successful Scrappy-Doos fighting crime (mainly metaphorically, but in some cases literally) in corporate hierarchies the world over. They work hard all of the time, battle for everything, and then wag their little tails whenever Uncle, or Auntie, Scooby gives them a cookie. And bosses love them for it. Note also that scrappies may be bright and capable, but this is certainly not a requirement for moderately – in some cases hugely - successful Scrappy-hood, however exhausting it may be.

The karmic corporate employee must learn to smile inwardly at these cartoon antics. On one level they are childish, but they can also be a highly effective route to advancement under the protective wing, or paw, of Auntie Scoob. So we immediately come to a second central theme of this book: envy.

Now taking pride in one's work is a great thing, and without a bit of envy to go with it, many of us might start to question the value of getting up in the morning. At the very least, sales of higher-end personal grooming products would surely plummet.

But when 50- or 60-hour work weeks are normal, with emails and texts into the evening, and Twitter to keep an eye on too, it is hard not to develop a resentful streak regarding the Scrappies, Scoobies and indeed anyone else who seems to be ascending the corporate ladder at a faster pace than oneself. This way madness lies.

From envy to action

So here are a couple of simple techniques for dealing with envy and resentment as you feel them starting to build. In our experience the trick is to <u>act immediately</u> to let the poison out, because festering jealousy is a bitter and bilious potion.

Tip 1 – Create an anger email address ... and use it

You could set up <u>venomous.thoughts@hotmail.com</u> as the recipient address for your bile. But we are fairly sure that this one is already taken! Use your imagination, but the key point is that **only you** must have the password to this account! Once it's set up, you can safely fire off your feelings when the need arises, to be laughed at and deleted later on in the comfort of your own home with a glass of wine in hand.

As an additional safety measure for the cyber-paranoid, or if Scrappy happens to work in IT, you may need to permanently delete these emails from your office out-box after sending. But this is a detail that, in our experience, only mildly attenuates the soothing cathartic effect of releasing some pent up emotion into electronic oblivion.

Plus, think of all the problems you have avoided by not sending some ridiculous venting email directly to colleagues that you would only live to regret...

Tip 2 – Write it down so you don't have to say it

The snail mail equivalent comes into play if you are sitting in a meeting full of garrulous scrappies. They may not know what they are talking about, the objective of the meeting may not be clear, but that will not stop them from yapping. Yapping is, after all, the Scrappy way.

Even the most karmic corporate co-traveller can find these experiences tiring when repeated too often and in too similar a fashion. And it only takes a broken washing machine or a difficult morning school run to put you into just that place where you might break your Zen calm. This could lead to you doing something truly unwise, like speaking honestly and informing the room just how pointless this particular gathering is.

But out is better than in. Repression constipates. And constipation is not cool. If e-mailing in meetings is accepted in your organisation, you may need look no further than shooting off a rasping missive to "venomous.thoughts".

Alternatively, you can go old-school and simply write down your feelings on a sheet of paper. It will just look like you are taking a few notes. Plus you get the added pleasure of ripping the papers to shreds after your meeting has finished.

Tip 3 - There is no cure for pride and envy

Nor should there be. They are normal parts of the human psyche. The challenge for the karmic co-worker is simply to marshal these emotions in order to hit deadlines when needed and to generate some drive, rather than being ruled by them and pushed into full corporate prostration.

You'll only end up with a stomach ulcer.

The trickiest part of the art of self-ego management is that you can't flaunt it too publicly, and especially not to the chiefs. Even in the most enlightened organisations, managers need to generate ambition and purpose in their underlings: poking pride and envy inevitably become part of the policy mix.

Any whiff of sedition by not playing along with their game, however benign its intention, will certainly be picked up and quite possibly lead to a punishment of some sort. So be discreet.

To help you on your clandestine mission, Lucy Kellaway, the Financial Times columnist and one of the sources of inspiration for this book, developed the concept of the "office spouse" in one of her regular Monday articles on life in the modern corporate workplace.

The office spouse is a long-term office friend with whom you can exchange gossip, ideas and generally de-stress. But Lucy has worked in the same, relatively high-internal trust, newspaper environment for the last 25 years.

If, on the other hand, your working environment involves swimming with sharks on a daily basis, then we would err on the side of an extra private e-mail address and glass of wine once the kids are in bed.

You'll figure out what works best for you.

2. Should I stay or should I go?

If you've picked up this book, then the chances are that you are not completely happy with your current job. It probably isn't the worst job you've ever done or could imagine doing, but there are at least a few things that could be improved. This puts you in a tiny minority that includes nearly every other corporate worker on the planet.

But knowing that you are not alone does not help you to work out whether you need to take some action or just stick it out for a while longer in the hope that things will improve.

There is a nice story about the Head of the Business Decisions Division in a large consultancy firm who was agonising over lunch with a friend about whether to move to a position at a rival company. His friend, a lawyer, said: "Look, this is a business decision, surely your professional expertise should tell you how to analyse the problem?" "Yes", replied the executive, "but this is serious".

We have come across many models, plans and theories for optimal decision making and yet we still generally prefer simple rules of thumb. Charles Darwin's chosen method was to draw a line down the middle of a piece of paper and write the arguments in favour in one column and the arguments against in the other. But that was way back in the 19th century. Things have moved on massively since.

Tip 4 – How to rate your current job

First, draw a line down the middle of a sheet of paper. Second, in the left-hand column, write these three phrases:

- Do I respect the people I work for?

- Do I respect the people I work with?

- Do I work on things that I find interesting?

Third, after an appropriate period of reflection, answer each question by putting a score between "1" (yes) and "0" (no) in the right-hand column. Now add up your total score (hint: the result should be between 0 and 3). That's it.

If your score is significantly above 2, then you can probably give this book to a friend and stay put where you are. If you scored less than 1, you should start arranging some coffees and lunches with your best contacts pronto (on which more later). And if, like most people, you are somewhere in the middle, then we suggest that you stick with us for a little while longer so that we can help you to refine your ideas.

The first point we want to make here is that moving may not necessarily mean changing industry, apartment, spouse and country of residence all in one go. Based on extensive field research in company restaurants and cafeterias the world over, we can confidently report that the scores in our test vary enormously even <u>within</u> the same organisation, and often even within the same department. The test is useful because it's personal to you.

This is because so much depends on people, and all people are political (small p). Factions, tribes, sub-groups and splinter groups have been around since before the People's Popular Front of Judea developed their specific doctrinal shift. And they are here to stay. So we can't tell you whether to go to accounts, marketing or sales, but we can help you to work out whether it's time to make a move.

The second point is that all major change is stressful on some level. We reckon that we've developed quite a few of the tips in this book based on our own experience, but sometimes you just have to acknowledge that someone else got there first. Here it's the Swiss psychiatrist Elisabeth Kübler-Ross who published her famous work on the human psychology of grief in the late 1960s.

Tip 5 –Denial, Anger, Bargaining, Depression, Acceptance

The only thing that you need to do regarding this tip is to remember it (which is often easier said than done in times of high stress). Kübler-Ross was studying how humans respond to the extreme distress of death and dying and she defined five phases, which people experience in sequence:

- **Denial**: in which people flatly reject what has happened.

- **Anger**: in which frustration at the situation boils over.

- **Bargaining**: in which people try to find a way out, however fanciful.

- **Depression**: when the truth starts to hit home.

- **Acceptance**: when you can start to move on again.

The work has since been extended and various authors agree that the same simple model can be applied to virtually all cases of major change in people's lives. Most circumstances – thankfully - don't take as long to resolve psychologically as deep grief, but it's worth remembering that if you just got a terrible new boss, or if your beloved project has suddenly been taken from you and given to a colleague, it may take a bit of time before you can think straight.

Tip 6 – Don't make plans when you're tired or hungry

Most, if not all, human beings are capable of making terrible decisions if the prevailing context is not propitious. Elisabeth Kübler-Ross's central insight was to go easy on yourself if you are angry or depressed. We further recommend a Kit Kat and a cup of tea, perhaps preceded by a couple of good nights of sleep, to aid the process.

Thus equipped to analyse your situation and think about what to do next (including staying put, or moving just along the corridor), we're ready to look at a few more karmic corporate lifestyle tweaks.

3. Getting in

The main purpose of this book is to help people to thrive within, rather than strive to enter, corporate hierarchies. Many bookshelves are already lined with manuals on CV and interview techniques and our own skills are somewhat rusty. Nonetheless, we thought we'd better include a short section on interviews given that this will probably be an important element of any plan you may hatch to move on from a position that isn't up to scratch.

Tip 7 – Well-trained, well-educated, enthusiastic

We may be woefully out of date, but we struggle to improve much on the ancient advice on how to succeed in an Oxbridge interview. Well-trained means you know your stuff. Well-educated means you have some breadth, knowledge of the world, and at least an inkling of the social skills you'll need to get on over time. We can't teach you these things here, but any good interviewer will certainly test them.

And then comes the kicker. Enthusiastic sounds like the easy one. Don't be so easily fooled. As a little test, try recommending *with real enthusiasm to* a good friend to go and see a movie, or to read a book, that you hated. How did it go? Alternatively, just sit and watch them try to do same thing with a mutual friend when the three of you next meet up for a drink.

It turns out that feigning enthusiasm that you don't genuinely feel is very difficult, unless that is you're a highly-skilled actor or have the misfortune to be suffering from a psychotic condition.

This, by the way, is one reason why you tend to find out much more about people's true personality in high-stress situations. It's much harder to lie when you are in state of high emotional engagement. Or, to put it another way, not all diplomats were born ice-cool.

And this is why enthusiasm is such a powerful selection tool. Most interviewers want the person opposite them to *genuinely* want the job, for the simple and rational reason that an enthusiastic applicant is likely to work much harder if they are subsequently given the position.

There is some implicit karmic guidance in all of this. We are certainly not saying that you need to deliver an Oscar acceptance speech the next time you are interviewed for a job. But thinking about how much enthusiasm you can credibly convey is a good test of what your real emotions are likely to be when doing the job itself.

Happiness, after all, is mainly about living in phase with your values and emotions. So we reckon that the enthusiasm test is more significant than it might seem at first glance.

Oh, and don't forget to polish your shoes and read the morning papers.

4. Starting well

Sometimes the Scrappy-Doo way is the only the way. There is no use envying the woman in the corner office when you first arrive or being too proud to get stuck in and do some of the dirty work. You just have to roll up your sleeves and get started. For all eyes are on you at this moment, even if you are not aware of it.

Tip 8 – Your first piece of work is crucial

Psychologists claim that once we have formed a first impression of someone's personality type, it takes over 100 specific examples of contrary behaviour to change that impression. Life is definitely not fair. The upside, however, is that if you can start off well, you've created a tail-wind to help you to get up and running swiftly.

So the first time that you do a piece of work for a new boss or someone important in the organisation, it is imperative that you do it well. This may involve some Scrappy-Dooing.

Thinking can only get you so far in this world. Hard work and good fortune are just as important. So if you need to burn the midnight oil or miss a couple of bed-time stories to get off on the right foot with your colleagues, then just do it, it's a corporate karmic investment that will pay off.

Tip 9 – Walking should precede running

As any toddler quickly learns, doing things in the right order is important. You had to learn to walk before you could run back then and things haven't really changed since.

This is particularly difficult for our good friend Scrappy. So certain is he of his powers, and so strong is his hunger for a cookie and a pat on the head, that he is liable from the get-go to bound headlong into all sorts of power lines that he never even imagined could exist. Let him, by the way. There will be no thanks and no reward for saving him.

But if you can reign in your enthusiasm enough to observe who knows whom, who has been around forever, who the boss takes for lunch now and then, and how long it takes before you are invited for a drink - or whatever the ritual may be - with the team, then once again your karmic investment will pay a long stream of future dividends.

For these are some of the keys to knowing where the real power lies.

It is therefore far better to learn that Jenny, the mildly autistic senior manager, relies on Geoff, the stalwart of the IT department, for essential office gossip <u>before</u> you scream down the phone that someone needs to come and fix the printer immediately so that you can meet an urgent deadline. For example.

5. Getting noticed

Thus having avoided total career meltdown from day one and with a few decent pieces of work under your belt, it is time to turn to getting on a bit. Karmically, of course.

Tip 10 – Bosses will steal your ideas, it's what they do

One of us was once sat in a restricted, formal meeting of very senior diplomats* in which a French* official was complaining about how a high-ranking Indian* counterpart had done the dirty on him by "stealing" some ideas they had discussed privately in the midst of a very sensitive negotiation.

Now all cultures have strengths, but when it comes to straight-talking feedback, Finns are in a class of their own. After the complainant had finished, the Finnish Ambassador* gently pressed the button on his microphone, turned to his colleague and said: "It's life, get over it".

We are, of course, right back to the recurring theme of personal pride. For, as we have already seen, it is one of the central means by which large organisations perform the daily miracle of getting intelligent people to give away their best ideas for the good of the company.

Because this is what you will be doing – in return for salary and benefits, naturally.

This can come as a shock to some. It is, after all, only natural to feel some resentment towards a boss who gives a presentation you have prepared, or who does not copy you in on that strategic email to the top brass over which you have been agonising for weeks.

Read on for a few tricks that you can deploy to try to avoid this happening too often, but when it does occur, because it will, think back to the Frenchman*, the Indian* and the Finnish Ambassador*. And maybe fire off an email to "venomous.thoughts". It works for us.

Tip 11 – Truth is bilateral

Once you have accepted that your ideas *will* be stolen (for a pre- agreed monthly fee, hopefully with healthcare included) you can focus on the karmic task of influencing *how* and *when* this is most likely to occur.

Unless you are the boss, in almost all organisations, it is a cardinal sin to have good ideas in public, by which we mean in meetings with a mixture of juniors and seniors present. The <u>only</u> exception is if you have pre-briefed your bosses accordingly.

The go-to guru on this issue is Sheldon Cooper's mother. For those of you too busy to be familiar with the "Big Bang Theory", Sheldon is – in the hit comedy series - a theoretical physicist with an IQ of 187 and the catchphrase "I'm not insane, my mother had me tested".

Well, Sheldon's mother's savvy does not stop there. One of her great, and repeated, lines to her son is that: "You've got to stop doing that 'showing everyone else how much smarter than them you are all the time' thing". When a puzzled son asks why, Sheldon's mother fires back the immortal truth: "Because people just don't like it".

In corporate life it is less painful all round to learn from observing other people's mistakes rather than from making your own. So let Sheldon's mother be your guide. If you are going to go to the trouble of having good ideas on a regular basis, you'd be well advised to see things through to the end and think just as carefully about how you communicate them to the holders of power.

Tip 11 the hard way – Gyms, clubs and dinner parties

Just in case you haven't grasped it already, we're going to spell it out for you. If you want to get noticed for having good ideas rather than the ability to simply work harder and take more pain than your colleagues, then you are going to need to find a way to communicate to your bosses <u>in private</u>.

This is inherently somewhat seditious, and so, once again, you need to exercise caution and restraint.

The old-fashioned advice is to work out where the bosses hang out and then join them. But in our experience there is always a tedious *quid pro quo*. The associated ritual humiliations can come in many forms. It may mean having to lose repeatedly to your manager at squash, your partner having to endure a goading over dinner by the ultimately deeply insecure and frustrated boss's partner, or joining some hugely over-priced health club in the hope of bumping into the Chief Executive at the water fountain.

Now we have conducted some research that shows that regular exercise with a given colleague can lead to trust-building (see next chapter). A member of our Sangha (see tip 35 in chapter 13) was even willing to endure a series of spinning sessions to test out this theory. But after long discussions, she is willing to accept that this only really works with one's peers.

In any social situation that you have engineered with your hierarchical seniors, the boss will always require you to endure some ceremony of self-sacrifice before they will grant you your five-minute private audience in which to present your idea. And then you always run the risk that they are hung-over, not in the mood, or just don't like the look of your face.

Tip 11 in the 21st century – The Sunday morning email

Technology can be a menace, but it also has upsides. Whilst many corporate titans are addicted to their Blackberries and iPhones, constantly checking them for signs of the next threat to the share price, it is certainly the case that no serious corporate boss can spend a whole weekend without reading their emails.

Now maybe there exist some hyper-wired organisations in which everyone is "on it" 24/7 and no time of any day or night is sacred any more. Our sense is that in these places, Donald Trumps only need apply. For they have forsaken any scope for karma whatsoever. As we indicated in the introduction, if blood and the chance for honour are your only motivational drivers, then pick up one of the many luridly coloured books with capitalised titles on "winning" and "leadership" the next time you are in an airport bookshop. Our vision is different.

For the karmic corporate employee seeks and identifies niches, and we know of enough organisations in which the pace of electronic life slows at the weekend to think that we have a neat short-cut for you: the Sunday morning email.

You don't have to write it on a Sunday, you don't in general have to work on Sundays, but an email sent at around 11.30 on a Sunday morning should be read by most bosses on Sunday afternoon, just around the time when they are thinking about how to structure the next week, or maybe even the next few months, of business activity.

Most senior managers spend far too much time in meetings and have a lot less discretionary time than they would like. They also like to appear clever, but have too little time to think seriously and strategically about the business because in real life people fall ill, make mistakes, cheat, lie and get up to all manner of things that need to be, for want of a better word, managed. Even Donald finds this tiring, on occasion, or so we are told.

So late Sunday morning is your window for a crisply-worded, introductory email with one simple attachment sent straight to the power centre. They might not respond immediately to your initiative, but we guarantee they will read it and, quite possibly, think about it.

And they too will probably be relieved that they didn't have to work up a sweat on a squash court, argue with their partner about dinner menus and seating arrangements, or get irritated by some over-enthusiastic underling at the one sanctuary they have managed to arrange for themselves: their super-expensive health club.

The very worst that can happen is that your idea gets pinched for free with no direct feedback or reward. But then that was pretty much what was going to happen anyway.

Classical Karma

6. Building trust

If you have read this far, then you are probably open to some of the more subtle techniques that we have been advocating for getting settled-in and established in your corporate environment. In spite of all the guff that gets spouted about the importance of "information sessions for newcomers" and "helping you to get started quickly", you probably didn't receive that much useful advice from serious colleagues at the beginning. After all, serious people tend to want something in return.

But having done some useful work and established your place, you may become more "attractive" to colleagues who are willing to engage in some sharing and exchange of advice and ideas.

The acceptance rituals come in many forms, from drinks after work through lunchtime yoga groups to coffee clubs, but they matter. For they provide some counter-balance to the ever-present villains: envy and pride.

This chapter is probably not rocket science to anyone with reasonable social skills, but we have the impression that many younger colleagues have grown up in a more digitised age in which sharing a cup of tea and maybe even a cookie has zero relevance. Perhaps when our generation has retired this chapter can be permanently deleted from the updated E-reader version, but to the extent that those who have been around for a while have at least some useful things to pass on, we're happy to provide a few thoughts on how to access their knowledge.

Tip 12 – Find out what people like, then ask them about it

Friendships are built around common interests and experiences. Facebook is one route, apparently, but we're just not going to put anything seriously insightful there as the context is plain wrong.

Ask Mary* a thoughtful question over a cup of tea about improving your piano technique, however. Or share some web-links with William* that explain why, historically, Nottingham Forest are a better football (soccer) team than Leicester City. And you're flying.

A withering cynic might view this as manipulative behaviour, but it's just how people are. If you show repeated interest in their interests, then they are likely to be willing to share something useful with you in return. See it as purely transactional if you like, or see it as constructing a bit of social fabric. It's as you prefer, but it is surprisingly effective and possibly even rewarding. For the real point is that by demonstrating some awareness of the finer points of social interaction you are likely to spark the interest of people who are actually worth listening to. Scrappies need not apply.

Tip 13 – Always provide a pretext for them to decline

One older chap in our acquaintance once explained that "every gentleman should tolerate a mild, but chronic injury". By which he meant a pretext to refuse any unwanted social or sporting invitation.

Now you are probably too busy to read any more of this chapter right now, but, if not, then you really have no excuse (!).

The point is that serious people will tend to notice these little signifiers that you don't take a purely pre-Copernican view of your own personal relationship with the known universe. For they are indicative of a capacity to listen, to empathise even, and most people love to be listened to (a topic we will develop in the next chapter).

So, in simple terms, if you are trying to build on a Sunday morning email to arrange a one-to-one meeting with a more senior colleague, always phrase it in such a way that they have an easy way out ... "if you're not away on business that week ...", "if you are not tied up with the Chief Executive ..." etc etc. They may well choose not to exercise the get out clause, but they will certainly notice its presence.

Good manners and an appropriate dose of flattery are a surprisingly powerful combination.

Tip 14 – Keep in touch with people about as often as they keep in touch with you

No-one likes to be harangued and patience is a virtue. If someone hasn't responded to two or three emails full of your brilliant ideas, then the fourth will be a wasted bullet.

If, on the other hand, they do respond in a sincere and interested way, but take a while, then maybe they are politely indicating that they are more senior, or perhaps they have just been busy recently. Developing a feel for these things can take a bit of time, but the most important point is to notice the details – such as timing, font and size, indirect references... Because you can't factor in what you haven't grasped.

Tip 15 – The chiefs can only be frank in private too

The final point we want to make in this chapter is that any bilateral channel that you establish with one of the chiefs needs to be private for them too. One of the major challenges for corporate leaders is that everything they say and do ripples out across the organisation. As a result, anything from a poorly-timed joke to a frank remark taken out of context can do real harm.

The self-discipline that effective leadership requires over the long-term can make for quite a lonely experience. The point here is not to feel sympathy for the big chiefs but to recognise the risk that *they* are also taking if they start engaging frankly and in private with you.

Enjoy your badge of honour wisely.

7. Tuning in

There is an interesting passage in Malcolm Gladwell's book "Blink" about a marriage guidance counsellor who – as a result of years of experience of working with troubled couples – was able to spot within a matter of minutes those relationships that were beyond saving. The counsellor's knowledge in this regard could be boiled down to a single word: contempt. The more frequently that the counsellor observed contempt expressed between the unhappy couple, the more impossible his task became. Who are we to argue?

The opposite of contempt is respect. We strongly recommend that you keep a look out for contempt and respect in your professional (and personal) relationships. Just feel them. If you want to make a financial analogy: buy on respect, sell on contempt.

In our experience there is simply nothing to be gained from trying to work with people who are contemptuous towards you. Ever. Hopefully you don't feel this way about too many of your current colleagues either (if you do – see chapter 2), but if contempt is heavily present in either direction … "Houston, we have a problem".

Respect on the other hand is something worth cultivating and building. Like most of the higher things in life, no-one fully controls it, but since you probably spend more waking hours in the office than anywhere else – it's one of those things that's nice to have around.

Tip 16 – Listen to Epictetus

"We have two ears and one mouth so that we can listen twice as much as we speak." Thus spake the slave turned philosopher. Perhaps in the future we will evolve third and fourth ears, but for now we are stuck with a mere two.

Because in many respects the more you listen the easier things get. More time spent listening means less time speaking and that means fewer mistakes, less mess to clean up and more time for learning how to do things properly. That's a rare example of a virtuous circle.

It also means you have more time to observe all of the little clues by which people reveal themselves, whether deliberately or not. The phrases that tell you where they come from, the clothes that tell you how highly they regard themselves, and the excessive use of make-up/ hair product that reveals her/ his fundamental insecurity.

Time to stop before it gets catty, but we'd like to close this chapter by confirming what you've suspected all along: the insecure are just as dangerous as the contemptuous if not more so. If you are mainly calm and relatively grounded, the deeply insecure will hate you. Just sayin'.

8. Getting your point across

Well, if you've read this far, we must have at least some credibility on the issue. The preceding chapter was all about learning how to shut up, which in our experience is the essential pre-requisite for learning how to speak effectively. Why? For the same reason that it is a rare chef indeed who does not enjoy eating good food. Born orators aside, the better you are at listening, the better you will be at presenting your ideas. Because you know what it's like to sit in the audience.

Tip 17 – The importance of being structured

There are some differences between good writing and effective speaking, but structure is one thing they certainly have in common. If you haven't come across or have since forgotten the old adage on essay writing: "tell 'em what you're gonna tell 'em; tell 'em; tell 'em what you've told 'em", then download it to your hard-drive right now.

Because it amazes us how often even experienced public speakers forget this simple trick.

It would be lovely to think that the real challenge with an audience is getting them to remember all of your main points. Sadly, it's actually about trying to get them to pay attention to any of them.

When you open your mouth in public you are essentially engaging in a cage-wrestling fight to the death with e-mails, texts, Twitter and Candy Crush in a tag-team with the hopelessness of human short-term memory on one side, versus your own personal charisma on the other.

But we are karmic. We understand that the average human being can keep no more than six points in her short-term memory bank at any given time. We also know that there does exist a small proportion of our species which has engaged with and developed its own "mind palace" and can "storify" information in such a way as to massively increase the potential of their short-term memory way beyond the average six items. Google it if you don't believe us.

But sadly none of these people are going to be attending your fifteen-minute (less is better, <u>never</u> agree to more) slot on "How to be a better accountant". We also know that three is half of six and it's better to be on the safe side. So here is what we suggest you do:

1. Stand up.

2. Start with a short personal anecdote if you possibly can

(Ideally your heart rate should now be back below 150)

3. Tell them the three points you are going to make.

4. Illustrate those three points in the form of three short "stories".

5. Recall the three points you have made.

6. Sit down. Observe that some of the audience are still awake.

Smile.

9. Saying no without putting people off

We are not, as a general rule, in favour of jokes that contain even the slightest bit of sexism, nor any other kind of unacceptable prejudice for that matter. But the fact is that if you are competent and able more or less to act upon Chapters 1- 8, then you are going to be in high demand. And that may not be all it is cracked up to be.

So either skip the chapter, put a peg on your nose, or pause that Benny Hill YouTube retrospective and pay attention…

Question: how do you tell the difference between a diplomat and a lady?

Answer: If a diplomat says yes, he means maybe, if he says maybe he means no, and if he says no then you know he's not a diplomat … And (attaching peg) if a lady says no she means maybe, if she says maybe she means yes, and if she says yes, well then she's not a lady.

Noting our further slip towards the heteronormative abyss by having assigned traditional gender roles to the diplomat and the lady, what possible purpose could this unacceptable humour serve?

Well, to be blunt, if women are so good at avoiding the word yes in other areas of life, why are they often so bad at it in the office?

Two further qualifications are in order. First, this is not a relevant issue during your "start-up" phase in a new job. Then it's Scrappy-Doo to the max as discussed in chapter 4. Second, by women what we really mean are "competent, reasonable people". This is a category that actually includes many men (but we don't know of and couldn't find any jokes about competent, reasonable men) and excludes life-long female scrappies, of which there are plenty.

So what to do?

Tip 18 – Let me at 'em Uncle Scoob

Well, there is something to be said for the Scrappy-Doo method here too. Scrappies don't have a problem saying yes to everything because they immediately delegate it to others or forget about it altogether and move on to something else. This can be very effective and it's why scrappies aren't bad people as such, they're just dangerous to know if you generally hang with the calm and competent crew.

There may be a problem, however, with attempting to selectively adopt *some* Scrappy habits. The challenge is posed by the other scrappies in your organisation. For they operate according to scent and instinct and will quickly be onto you. Dogs are hierarchical pack animals and lone wolves are, well, let's just say it's not a label we think you should be aiming for.

So once you start playing by, even some, canine rules, it's likely you'll need to be ready for a series of dogfights to establish your place in the rankings. A position you will then need to fight to maintain.

Note also that pack rankings do not necessarily follow the formal hierarchical job titles according to which people get paid. Every pack has lore of its own.

So keeping a couple of sword lengths away from the madding crowd may be good for your karmic state, but won't it mean missing out on some of the projects and promotions that might interest you?

An honest assessment of the current state of karmic wisdom obliges us to answer that sometimes, yes. Unless you are willing to fight like a dog on a daily basis, then we think that you can still expect corporate progress, but you may need to have a bit of extra patience.

Every approach to life has its weaknesses and this is one of ours – unless maybe you can help? We have personally never figured out how to have our cake and eat it in this respect. But maybe there are mutants out there who are further along the evolutionary chain? If you do manage sustainably to combine workplace karmic thoughtfulness with Scrappy-Doo delegation antics, please write to us and tell us how it's done, and we'll give you a hat-tip one way or the other, promise.

Tip 19 – Keep your word, in the fullness of time

Karmic life is four-dimensional: height, width, depth plus … duration. For us, not everything has to be immediate. Waiting a minute or two need not be a sign of weakness. Indeed, silence is not only golden, it is one of the most powerful moves in the karmic playbook. As all military recruits soon learn …

Sergeant (to a group of privates): "Right, men, who likes ice-cream?"

Fresh-faced private: "Me, sir."

Sergeant: "Excellent, Richards, you're on duty tonight."

The capacity to keep quiet is a magic recipe for avoiding a great deal of wasted effort. But just think of Scrappy's torment. He knows the answer. He's desperate for his cookie. He just can't hold it in. If only he could think <u>before</u> speaking. What a gift that would be.

Given that this aspect of corporate karma rewards both creativity and a sense of playfulness, let's take a brief look into the history of the office and see how our karmic forebears did it. With the current trend towards cramped, open-plan offices (on which more later) some of the higher-end arts of slowing things down to a more appropriate pace have fallen into disuse.

This is a pity. Because <u>door management</u> was once one of the finer examples of how to reveal a taste for ice-cream, but only in the fullness of time.

For anyone too young to have worked in a cellular office set-up, a wide open door serves as an invitation to sergeants of all stripes to stride in with fresh commands. A door left only a fraction ajar, however, inserts a minimum of doubt into the mind of the moustachioed menace. Should she knock?

For it is just possible that one of her seniors is lurking on the other side of the Rubicon. Or should she simply avoid the risk by going to the next (wide open) door?

Lost too are many of the works by artists drawn to this particular medium. The "defective" coat hook fixed to the back of one's office door. The worn-out "spare office coat" to hang upon it, of just the right weight to fall to the floor of its own accord, and of just the right thickness to jam the door if opened "inappropriately". Halcyon days.

The modern-day executive must make do with being a trifle more direct, but need show no lesser degree of cunning.

A simple and pleasing technique when Sergeant Scrappy next fires an instruction in your direction is to ask her immediately to confirm that this needs to be checked with Head Office/ as a minimum someone who does not work in direct line of sight of where your conversation is taking place. If Scrappy asks you why, reply that four eyes see more than two, or something similarly trite but unarguable.

Scrappy is probably already getting bored by now and given that you haven't said no, may even forget to set you a deadline (assuming that she has the power to do so).

And so you can then duly reply to her, as you should, and, indeed, must, for it is karmic to keep one's word – trust matters a great deal. But in the fullness of time. Because everyone knows that it often takes a few days to get hold of the right person at Head Office.

You get the point.

Tip 20 – Manage your own deadlines and always appear busy

The central message here is that deadline management is simply far too important for thoughtful executives to delegate upwards to their hierarchical seniors. Keep your own deadlines firmly within your secretly vice-like grip.

Another key consideration is that you must always appear busy. There is little more palliative to the fervent Scrappy mind than the apparent toil of others. Points for artistic merit may be awarded to those who periodically "fail" to properly replace their telephone handsets or who block chunks of their electronic calendars with "busy" periods and "restricted" meetings.

Because everyone needs a bit of time to think.

Tip 21 – Gold stars are for school children

The final ingredient is to free yourself from the chains of positive feedback. We all like a bit of sincere praise, but gold stars are for school children.

There is nothing more damaging to the perspective of corporate karma than the irrepressible need for an A-grade on every project. Let it go. It's the fundamental difference between you and Scrappy. She always wants and needs a cookie. You don't.

Or think of it as akin to that moment when you realised that there was simply no point trying to fulfil all of your parents' expectations. Because impossible means what it says on the tin.

But you still love your parents. And you can certainly love your job too.

10. Pay attention to your environment

Here's a question. What proportion of the general adult population do you think is capable of sadistic violence? Behavioural psychologists used to think there was an easy way to find out the answer. First, look up how many people are convicted of violent crimes each year. Second, factor in some survey evidence given that not all violent crimes are reported. Third, divide the number you reach by the overall size of the adult population. This would typically give a figure reassuringly below 1 or 2 per cent. This is equivalent to a peace-loving 98 or 99 per cent. Sounds about right, doesn't it?

But what if this is not the full story?

A famous experiment conducted in the US in the early 1970s, the so-called "Stanford prison experiment", took a group of university students who had been rigorously tested and interviewed to ensure that they were not suffering from any psychological disorders and had never been convicted of any violent offences.

It then placed them in a confined building and asked them to live together. The only twist was that half of the students were dressed in law-officer uniforms and the others were dressed as prisoners.

To cut a long story short, the experiment had to be abandoned after only a few days as a result of punishment beatings meted out by the "police" on the unruly "prisoners". That 1 or 2 per cent figure started to look a bit shakier. It turns out that context matters. And by a lot more than you would like to think.

Now we seriously hope that you do not encounter actual physical violence in your workplace. That is not a matter for chapter 2 but for the real police and legal authorities.

But the point that we want to get across is that your workplace environment is important. Very important, in fact. Because the setting in which you work frames what is deemed to be acceptable and what is not.

We discussed door management in the last chapter. This chapter is about much more than merely avoiding eye contact with Scrappy-Doo at inconvenient moments.

As we began to explore in the last chapter, a typical modern-day office lay-out has been designed by scrappies for scrappies. Open spaces, desks close together, walls removed unless essential for structural support.

This creates a noisy, shouty, bustling dynamic. Ideal if you are selling tomatoes on a market, or looking to rapidly offload a fresh set of requests from the chief onto a group of underlings.

But what if you are trying to work out the optimal transfer price for an input in a global product supply chain? Or drafting a recommendation about whether to grant early release to a convicted criminal with a positive record of good prison behaviour. People who work in open-plan corporate and government offices do this sort of thing every day.

The trick here surely is finding a decent balance. Many scrappies are loveable really and effortlessly generate both infectious energy and a continuum of bad ideas for us to re-shape (just kidding, scrappies!). Without them, their karmic colleagues might not have jobs!

Equally, too much karma might lead to quasi-monastic conditions. Now monasteries do seem to have been a propitious environment down the centuries for the production of beer, herbs and scripture. But they can also be a bit draughty and few of us want to start work before dawn every morning.

More operationally, there is an interesting section in a recent book, "Quiet" by Susan Cain, about finding one's own optimal level of work-place stimulation. By this she means things like the level of background noise, proximity to colleagues and frequency of meetings.

It turns out that there are huge differences between people. Some like it "hot" in the sense of multiple parallel sources of stimulation, whereas other are a bit "cooler".

Tip 22 – Know your sweet spot and try to get close to it

It may take some time before you have figured out whether you prefer open plan or a cubicle, daily brainstorming or occasional team retreats. There is no one-size-fits-all policy and life would be less interesting if there were. The important point for karmic corporate living over the medium-term is that you work out what suits you and find something that approximates to it.

Most market traders would probably be bored in a monastery and there aren't many monks dealing blackjack in Vegas, at least as far as we know. So follow the Delphic maxim: know thyself.

In recent decades, pressures towards cost-saving and quick solutions have tended to narrow the physical gaps between employees as walls and partitions have given way to large open spaces. Yet the traffic has not been all one way.

Quiet areas, reading rooms and private phone booths are often installed for those who need them. Plus the scope to move between noisier and quieter areas of an office space can facilitate a much-needed change of scene if you're stuck on some specific work problem. So with any luck, over time you'll be able to find your corporate niche both literally and organisationally.

And if things get desperate, you can always resort to the quasi-military response of an ageing researcher* in our acquaintance when informed that his team was being moved to an open-plan office. He stood up to his full height and proudly announced: "Colleagues, we shall build walls with our books".

Tip 23 – Idle hands make the devil's work

The last point in this chapter is that we hope you don't think we are advocating laziness. Lazy colleagues with too little work to do are best avoided. Give us scrappies instead every time. In our experience, it's much more stimulating all round to be surrounded by capable, hard-working colleagues and to contribute actively to that vibe. More broadly, we have observed that "good" people tend to work in the busier parts of respected organisations. By all means join them.

Our objective is simply to help you to distinguish between quality and volume. Between efficient decision-makers and those who are merely flying by the seat of their pants.

Ultimately, we are back to the issue of mutual respect between colleagues. It may sound very old-fashioned, but as we argued in chapter 2, we reckon it's equivalent to roughly two-thirds of your overall job satisfaction. So it's worth looking out for.

11. Setting the agenda

Many areas of life are unfair and it is karmic to recognise and accept this, however hard it may be at times. Large modern organisations are rarely bastions of (corporate, or any other type of) justice for all of the reasons we have been discussing in this book. The main factor is that it generally pays off at the margin to be unreasonably aggressive and "macho". Energy displayed, however ill-focused, is sadly much easier for management to reward than good judgement assiduously practised.

But there is surely one great exception to this tide of iniquity, a phenomenon so subtle in its evolution that it absorbs large amounts of even the most alert Scrappy's time. And which thus, no matter how nefarious it may at first appear, serves - at least temporarily – to free the thoughtful from the shackles of wanton delegation to reflect and create in peace.

What is this mystical beast? What name is carried by this monster that stalks the corridors, offices and open-plan spaces of Corporationia with such blatant disregard for the upper echelons?

In most organisations, it is known simply as: the meeting.

For what could be more tedious? Perhaps the first few times one attends a meeting there is, akin to the first time one engages in any new activity, a certain fascination in grasping the rites and rituals. There may even be an adrenalin rush to enjoy in advance of "taking the floor". But surely even the most ego-centric careerist must tire rapidly, not only of the hackneyed platitudes trotted out by his colleagues, but even of his own modulated vocabulary in this rather formalised setting? Although where scrappies are concerned, we still harbour some major doubts...

As we have seen in chapter 5, meetings are rarely the appropriate occasion for bright ideas or insightful comments, unless the brass has been duly warned in advance, of course. And yet meetings are senior managers' second homes. A vortex from which few manage to escape.

In a world of man-made climate change, the Gaia thesis, with its leaning towards self-regulatory and spontaneous counter-reactions to destabilising events, has rather fallen out of fashion. And yet what more elegant, organic response to a corporate environment excessively dominated by the congenitally aggressive could one possibly conceive of than the humble meeting?

Like some magnificent pair of metaphysical lungs, meetings conceptually suck in the garrulous, groupings them into rings of energetic activity, and then exhale their blustery output into the great winds of eternity.

This "pressure-release" function of the meeting ought never to be under-estimated. For we must be consistent. We said in chapter 1 that out is better than in when we advocated an email to "venomous.thoughts" for all those of karmic sensibility needing to release a build-up of bilious envy.

Scrappies need their outlets too. They have their rights and, being scrappies, they prefer public to private fora. Enter the meeting.

To be clear, what we mean by a meeting is any gathering of between say 6 and 20 or so people around a single table. These might typically be called "board" or "management" meetings in many organisations. We will come to "small groups" (in which productive interaction between participants may sometimes be possible) and "large gatherings" (where it most certainly is not) in a moment. Let's start in the middle.

Neophytes may be forgiven for thinking that the main objective of this kind of "middle-sized" meeting is to come up with new initiatives and take decisions. Nonsense. Apart from in a genuine emergency, the decisions have already been taken before the meeting starts based on ideas dreamt up weeks ago.

Meetings essentially exist to <u>legitimise</u> decisions and to offer a <u>parade ground</u> for the victorious.

But they also achieve much more. As so often, the <u>semiotics</u> of the environment are more telling than the words that are spoken. Boardroom tables are generally oval or rectangular. When fully attended, a boardroom creates a "wall of backs" to outsiders. Meetings of this size are all about whether you are "in" or "out". They serve to create an insider group of "decision-makers" who develop internal codes and rituals of their own.

But don't many meetings go on for hours? How can this be rational, sensible or efficient in a competitive global marketplace? Slowly, doth the mysteries of the universe reveal themselves.

Because as well as legitimising decisions, meetings create hours, days and weeks of free therapy for scrappies. They can argue to their hearts content about minor details of drafting and major elements of grand strategies that competent individuals below them will generally ignore. They can scheme with one another, undermine enemies, create new alliances and generally enjoy themselves. They also get to speak a fair amount which makes them feel important.

One of the great advantages of being a Scrappy is that, even though you care a lot about how you are *perceived*, you don't worry too much about whether or not what you say makes sense. This must be very liberating. And meetings provide the perfect forum for enjoying this particular form of freedom. Scrappies just need to make sure that they have the full and undivided canine support of whatever pack of players around the table they belong to. Provided this back-up is there, they are happy. And, in this sense, they are also extremely wise.

But what if you want to have a gathering that actually discusses something in detail? Then you need a small group…

Tip 24 – Never more than seven

Seven is pretty much the biggest number of people with whom you can have a proper discussion of an issue in which everyone gets to say what they think. Any more than seven present and you can be sure to have generated at least two factions and that will detract from the quality of debate. Six is better than seven and five better still.

But life is about imperfect compromises, so do the best you can in the circumstances.

Tip 25 – Don't forget the cookies

The second point is that the rituals of "sitting down together" help. Bring tea and cookies. Don't sit in two rows facing one another. Form a circle or a semi-circle. Light a communal fire (metaphorically!) if you can. Now you're talking…

Tip 26 – A picture paints a thousand words

If you want to influence the outcome of this kind of gathering, remember that most people are poor listeners, with short attention spans who quite like talking too. So you could speak at length if you wish, but it may well be more effective to draw a simple picture illustrating what you mean. Let the others add a few lines to your sketch and, collectively, you will be close to completing the picture. Symbolically, at least.

This is also, by the way, an excellent and non-intrusive way of setting the agenda in a meeting with your seniors. Just come into the room with some <u>simple</u> sketch that represents your idea, or with three words written on a piece of paper visibly on top of your pile of documents. Curiosity gets the better of nearly everyone. "What's that?" they will ask. And in telling them, you have set the agenda for the conversation!

Tip 27 – Use the vocabulary of your approvals committee

One of us used to work for a boss who prized two qualities above all others: efficiency and vigilance. Now one of the benefits of abstract nouns is that they can legitimately be used to describe almost anything. And so it was that in any presentation of a new idea to said individual, the central objective would always be to enhance efficiency and the watchword vigilance. Approval became a matter of course. Try it, you might like it.

Tip 28 – It's the size of the audience, stupid

And so we finally turn to large group meetings. Here we have developed an iron-clad law: the amount of guff spouted at any given meeting is directly proportional to the number of people present.

You have been warned.

The reasons are in fact fairly rational. One of the other innate advantages of the Scrapster is that he tends not to be very good at coming up with original ideas. Fighting yes. Bullying yes. Working hard … in most cases. But true creativity is not his thing.

The inherent advantage is that if and when Scrappy does come across a good idea, he is loath to give it away.

Now put Scrappy in front of a roomful of several hundred executives, some of them from rival firms. Whilst karmic dreamers might be inclined to pass on some wisdom, Scrappy would never be so naïve.

He will therefore trot out whatever corporate starch his underlings have copy-pasted for him from previous similar engagements and not bat an eyelid when his fellow panellists do the same. Only if one of them should reveal a genuinely lucrative idea to the room will he note down (i) the idea, and (ii) that this person hasn't really understood the game at all.

12. Body language and its discontents

For the karmically inclined, probably the best thing about meetings is the scope that they offer as a laboratory for body language experimentation. It is, for example, inherently childish to set off ripples and rounds of applause at random moments, but it is not hard to do and you might enjoy trying it the next time you are stuck in an audience for a few hours (hint: if there are three of you and you stagger it slightly, you cannot fail).

Provided that you are able to shut out the background noise, meetings also turn out to be a surprisingly efficient environment for quiet thought and reflection: no interruptions from colleagues with questions, no phone calls (unless you are creating yourself a diversion – on which more later), and no emails ... unless, that is, scrolling through your iPhone in-box is the summit of your creative capacity.

A very experienced friend of ours actually ensures that he is "obliged" to sit in at least two "large" meetings of this kind per week so that he has some quiet time and space to think.

He has also developed a neat body language trick to ensure that he is not disturbed. It involves nodding his head up and down in symbolic agreement about once every 2 to 3 minutes. That's it. Just try it the next time you need to get some work done during a "meeting".

Tip 29: Entering the land of nod

For even the most insecure and yappy Scrappy, the occasional nod of agreement is more than enough unspoken approval and encouragement to go on speaking for another few minutes, time which you can then use as best you see fit. It is so simple and so powerful. A nod in the right direction if ever there was one.

It also massively reduces the chances that you will be singled out for a "punishment question" from Scrappy for reading your emails too visibly during the duration of her talk. A win-win-win.

Tip 30: Always walk, never run

Positive energy gets things done. But running is rarely necessary.

As we have been at pains to emphasise throughout this book, our agenda is not about work-dodging or laziness (although Scrappy will have to reach for the outer limits of her munificence to grasp and – eventually, we hope - accept this).

Rather it is about efficiency in the truest sense. Getting the maximum output for the minimum input needed. And a calm environment that supports creativity is crucial for at least some of the workforce. As we have already underlined, context matters.

Scrappies are therefore welcome to take clients out on boozy nights of lobbying and touting for business. But quieter, perhaps even ultimately more strategic, colleagues should not have to endure frequent shouting matches during office hours. For the simple reason that this kind of environment is not conducive to thinking carefully, which costs good ideas, hence sales, hence profits and so: it's just bad business.

Now maybe on an old-fashioned securities trading floor, in a newsroom during a crisis, or in a hospital emergency ward, running is sometimes necessary. But even there it should not become the norm, because tired people think more slowly and make more mistakes.

There is even a wonderful demonstration of this point in Daniel Kahneman's "Thinking fast and slow". Randomly selected students are asked to do a "hard sum" (17x34 is plenty hard enough):

(a)   whilst running;

(b)   when sitting still in a quiet room.

Even scrappies should not be shocked that group (a) takes longer to get to 578 than group (b). It turns out that even walking at an uncomfortably fast pace is enough to knock the mathematical mind off its stride (which can be useful to know if you are tall and even mildly unscrupulous). So the body language lesson is clear: stay within your speed limit.

Tip 31: On the laying on of hands

Airport manuals on "leadership" and treatises on neuro-linguistic programming are brim-full of advice on how to demonstrate "alpha dominance" by clasping your "opponent's" shoulder, showing him through the door before you, or laying your spare palm on the back of her outstretched hand when you shake paws for the first time.

This kind of stuff can be intimidating at first, especially to the uninitiated, but like all minor bullies Scrappy is just looking for a "flight" reaction. The quicker she understands that you are neither bothered nor impressed, the quicker she will move on to the next perceived minnow.

In some cultures (of a more Mediterranean bent, for example) ritual forearm, elbow and shoulder "tapping" has evolved as a quick and unspoken means (for men, essentially) to exchange non-verbal hierarchical signals before getting down to business.

In very simple terms the higher-up the relative "tap" on the arm, the greater the extent by which A (considers that he) outranks B. Getting this wrong can have costs in some southern European, and other more socially conservative, business contexts, so it can be useful to know about. But we still struggle to get really excited about it.

Traditionally, women have been excluded from these games for basic macho reasons. Some modern female bosses do go in for aping these boyish rituals, be we are not impressed. Because, typically, these dominance games are symptomatic of pride-based, hierarchical cultures. Which are generally not our favourites as they tend to reward blind loyalty over creativity. And men over women.

But the most important point for the karmic corporatist is to be able very rapidly to understand the context in which they are expected to operate and then to react/ adjust/ move on accordingly. Merely by observing pervasive use of aggressive body language, for example, you can quickly figure out that you are surrounded by insecure, proud and (probably) ambitious colleagues. That's a lot of useful information for very little effort.

Tip 32: There are limits

There are a few other passive aggressive techniques that can be useful to know: looking at someone's ear when they speak to you; shaking your head in public when they are speaking; arriving deliberately late to meetings and so on.

Our feeling: observe the ways of the dark side, but do not join them.

13. In the long run, we are all karmic

John Maynard Keynes took the view that all practical men are the slaves of some defunct economist. By this he meant that the good people of the world who either need, or contrive, to be busy all of the time have to get their ideas from somewhere other than their own brains. Because they have neither the time nor the inclination to stop first and think carefully.

He had scrappies in mind.

Tip 33: Draw two lines on a page (version 2)

There are very few of us indeed who will ever ascend to the intellectual heights of JMK. Our best tip if you aspire to be a strategist and thinker of his calibre is to be born with an astonishing gift. For the rest of us, there are, however, a few tricks that can help us to avoid wasting enormous amounts of time chasing phantoms down blind alleys. For the first step towards thinking strategically is to think strategically about what you are going to think about.

But once again let us follow our own advice (from chapter 11) and draw a picture lest we get too abstract. Darwin liked vertical lines. Keynes liked to draw his at right angles. But there'll be no deviation into the realms of supply, demand and monetary theory. Promise.

Simple picture number 1

Things that...	are important	aren't important
you can influence	Karma	Folly
you can't	Frustration	Fruitless

You might want to think about the economic consequences of peace. But even JMK probably found that frustrating at times. Devoting a lot of time effort to change what Barack Obama eats for breakfast would probably be fruitless (pardon the pun). And worrying too much about the details of your own cereal intake would almost certainly be folly.

Now there's nothing wrong with a weak pun from time to time, but if you want to get one (or even several) steps ahead of Scrappy and his pals, then you need to head for the top-left corner.

Because the vast majority of people never manage to stop and think for long enough to realise that they are simply not focusing their energy where it matters. This realisation is step 1.

Now we are certainly not suggesting that having gotten to first base you will be heading straight for the office of the Strategy Director to find your name emblazoned on the door. But it is the kind of thought process that may get you the chance to set out your ideas within its confines. So now how about second base?

Tip 34: Identify the landing zone

We can't always know how things are going to end. And sometimes we can only properly understand a problem through the process of trying to solve it.

But this is not how scrappies think. In the vast majority of cases they have such a strong need to make "some progress, any progress" immediately that they can't resist starting to hack away at the undergrowth to clear a path before they know which way the river is.

Simple picture number 2

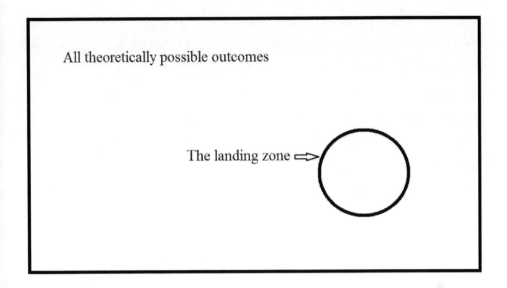

Following our own advice from chapter 11 for a second time in the space of barely a few pages, simple picture number 2 shows how to avoid Scrappy's second basic strategic error.

The key is, <u>first</u>, to think the problem through to the <u>end</u>, so you are sure that you know where you are trying to get <u>to</u>. Then, <u>second</u>, to work back from that destination to see what's stopping you from getting there <u>from</u> your starting point.

We prefer the term landing zone to destination, as it's probably more realistic to aim for one of a set of acceptable outcomes than to go for pin-point perfection. More broadly, the second part of the analysis process - working back from the landing zone - is usually hard. But that's ok, because most people don't even bother with the first part.

The best example of this that we have ever come across personally was when one of us got stranded in Sri Lanka just after Christmas 2004. For those with shorter memories, the Tsunami wave hit the east and south of the Island in the early morning of December 26th.

Our group was safe in the capital Colombo on the west of the island and so we tried to get involved and do a bit to help before finding a re-scheduled flight home. As a result we got to know a few of the basics of aid provision in a crisis from one of the seasoned old-pros who fly in to coordinate relief efforts when stuff like this happens.

We met him in a hotel bar in Colombo on the evening of December 27th 2004. He was having a beer and not looking too concerned.

"Why aren't you out delivering aid?" we asked.

"Bit early for that" he said.

"But there are injured people arriving in ambulances from the resorts on the south of the island".

"That's true, he said, but not many and anyway, I'm not a medic".

"How many medics have flown in then?" we asked.

"Not many", he said, "we actually don't expect there to be very many injured people."

"It may sound harsh", he continued, "but the people who got washed out to sea, drowned, and those who didn't generally aren't injured but will need food and shelter in the coming days."

"The weather's warm so exposure isn't a risk and we think that there are ample food and water supplies to last for at least a few days in most places, as it probably wasn't all washed away either."

"So why are you just sitting here having a beer?"

"It's my chance to get my thoughts together after a long flight. 'Cos at some point in the next few days I might go a day or two without sleeping."

"When that happens you need to have a plan in place that you can stick to when you get tired". (See tip 6 in chapter 2)

"So why aren't you shipping out all of the food that locals have donated? We've heard of Colombo people driving private convoys down south full of rice, water and clothes."

"You've more or less answered your own question. In a crisis like this, in the first few days, loads of small food and clothes parcels are donated by people who are happy just to be alive. That's fine, but it gets distributed to the places which are accessible."

"That's ok, isn't it?"

"Nothing wrong with it!"

"But?"

"But the question you've got to ask is: are the people in need in the places that are accessible?"

"We reckon that 60 – 70% of the people who'll start needing food and shelter soon are in the east of Sri Lanka. All the roads east from Colombo, where the aid will arrive, are currently blocked. So unless private volunteers have got private planes and helicopters – which they haven't - they're only addressing the easy part of the problem."

"Which suits us fine actually, 'cos we can then work with the Sri Lankan military to focus on the places that are hard to reach".

"They are much better and quicker at clearing roads than we can ever be, for example. They've got the kit and they've got the people."

"So once you've got a clear picture of where the needs are, then you'll start distributing the aid?"

"In principle."

"In principle?". He had a sip of his beer and leaned closer.

"You don't seem like idiots with big mouths and I can see that you mean well, so I'll let you into a little secret ... The first two planes full of international aid arrived around lunchtime today, but the cargo is still stuck in customs. It's Christmas, so most government officials and politicians were on holiday when the wave hit and some have lost family in the tragedy. It may take a day or two to start to get the aid cleared through the airport and onto trucks".

"Doesn't that frustrate you?"

"It's just one of those things in life that's important but that for now you can't do much about. My bosses know. The military knows. If there's no progress by tomorrow lunchtime then 'phone calls will start to be made by people with influence … But for now, I'll buy you a beer and then we should all try to get a good night's sleep".

If you're going to get taught a lesson, it's best to learn from a real pro.

Tip 35: The benefits of a Sangha

One of the biggest obstacles to keeping a clear head in difficult circumstances is that people panic. Even in normal types, nervous people often find it difficult to be around thoughtful types who prefer to let fools rush in where angels fear to tread.

There is a nice bit of simple Buddhist advice in this regard. It boils down to having a few like-minded friends. The Buddhist term is a Sangha. In other words, a small group of people with whom you can exchange ideas and from whom you know you'll get mutual support when the going gets tough. Something you can rely on.

We can't remember the name of the aid official that we met in Colombo in the hotel bar. But we like to think that if we did nothing else, we provided him with a temporary mini-Sangha before his real colleagues arrived to do the hard work of getting aid to Sri Lankans.

Jungle Boogie

14. Now for something completely different

Most cultures have their separation rituals. Gap years and Bar Mitzvahs seem relatively tame compared to the Amazonian tribe that sends its thirteen year-old boys off into the forest with the instruction not to return for at least ninety days to prove that they have learned the skills so essential to their survival.

The Amazonian way may sound harsh, but these are the kinds of people from whom Ray Mears gets his source material. For them it's not just enjoyable infotainment at 8pm on a Tuesday evening – it really is about putting speared fish on the table. So they need to know.

In any case, the point that all of these systems have in common is that there comes a time when you have to see whether the theory works in practice. Otherwise, why bother?

So returning to the harsh jungle of the modern corporate office environment, it's now time to leave safety of the village. There is a piece of graffiti in one of our local parks (in a very mixed, arty district, admittedly) that says: "real life starts where your comfort zone ends".

For us that means coffees, lunches, cocktails and dinner parties. You won't be needing the machete, but do try to keep your wits about you.

15. Coffee and repartee

We once came across a situation in which two scrappily ambitious Directors (both senior, but equal in rank) were supposed to meet to agree the way forward on a given issue. Their respective secretaries had both been trying to arrange a meeting for several weeks, but neither of the principals would agree to the meeting being held in the other's office. The symbolism was just too big an obstacle.

So the secretaries met for a cup of tea in the cafeteria and all of a sudden it came to them. They were just going to have to find a neutral venue.

This is the first point to grasp about a coffee invitation. It's a leveller. So if a more senior colleague invites you for a coffee, there's already a bit of kudos for you to enjoy quietly.

She's saying: let's go to a place where we can speak privately and (more or less) as equals, away from all of the hierarchical symbolism that even the most open-plan office will ritualise in some form or another.

By the way, we simply don't care about who gets the latest iPhone version the fastest where we work, but we are smart enough to realise that the order of distribution may convey important talismanic data.

Tip 36: Don't hang with the stingy or profoundly vain

Note also that if she is significantly more senior and has anything about her then she'll probably still insist on paying, as her little reminder that you shouldn't be too cheeky. And you should let her.

Moreover, if she's too tight to buy the coffee or deliberately turns up much more than ten minutes late in a vanity display, then you shouldn't rush to have coffee with her again because neither the stingy nor the profoundly vain merit any place in your Sangha.

And if she's prattling on and on with not the slightest intention to listen to any of your ideas: then don't forget, you can have another meeting to go to too.

But however inwardly annoyed you were and even if you needed to fire one off to "venomous.thoughts" as the caffeine hit was kicking in after the meeting, you have certainly not wasted your time. That 20-minute coffee was worth its weight in Gold Blend. Because now you know for sure that Madame Tight and Vain is to be treated politely, just like everyone else, but you should never expect anything from her and so there is no point investing in the relationship.

Or, in other words, she is simply not in your landing zone…

Tip 37: Beware of cookie monsters

If you've read this far into this book then, like we authors, you've also dabbled in the shiny airport books on "being the best leader you can be" *et cetera*. These tomes often emphasise *inter alia* that "leaders, like bankers, always pay for lunch" (i.e. such that the "recipient" owes them morally, as well as financially).

Now we are certainly not trying to overturn decades of conventional wisdom by heretically arguing that the "free lunch" does in fact exist (for more on this see the next chapter). And if ever you do happen to receive one, then it's by accident. But then accidents do happen, just ask anyone in the insurance business.

All we are really saying is that if you know your semiotics then you can neutralise a lot of the hidden aggression just by being aware of it.

In other words, Scrappy may get all het up about whether he invited you for coffee, who pays, and who arrives two emblematic minutes later than the other. But we are karmic, we are cool and we have Kindles (or even books!) in our pockets. So if Scrappy turns up ten minutes late, then you are already onto chapter 15 … Just don't give him eye contact until he actually comes over to your table and sits down. He's a really interesting guy, of course, but this book you're into is just such a riveting read.

That was a long introduction to cookie monsters, but then you've read (or might Google), your Friedrich Hundertwasser and so as well as knowing that he does curvy, shiny artwork, you have also grasped that the road to hell is typically deadly straight.

Cookie monsters, then, are people who will always buy some cookies to go with the coffee. Most things in life are rather grey than black or white, but cookie monsters come in two distinct categories: good and evil. And usually not in that order.

To make it very plain, Yoda will open the wrapper and put the cookies in the middle of the table. His message is: let us break bread together as friends (minus 20% for naïve optimism).

The Emperor, on the other hand, will subtly keep hold of the cookies, occasionally handing you one to enjoy. And usually after you have just agreed with him about something. His message: I am your master, but notice that I do reward my slaves with sweet treats when they show obedience. (See also wine-bottle keepers in the next chapter).

In Star Wars – with the notable exception of the Emperor himself - you don't need to be invited for a coffee to know the difference between a Jedi master and a Sith Lord. Sadly, in office wars, they dress the same, speak the same and operate from the same battleship. God is in the cookie-handling.

Tip 38: A coffee with a view

Really anal people of the sub-Emperor type will always insist on changing any table you may have chosen for your coffee in yet another demonstration of "alpha". Just laugh. And remember that other meeting in twenty minutes.

Worthwhile humans will however tend to notice if you have gone to the effort of selecting a table with some interesting paintings on a nearby wall or a nice view, for example.

And this matters. If your coffee is genuinely about exchanging ideas and thinking big, then it does actually help to be looking at a blue ocean or a bustling marketplace or an inspiring piece of art. Movement stimulates the conceptual mind.

In military terms, it also removes the adversarial aspect. A common enemy may be the most powerful stimulus to agreement, but a common friend rarely does any harm.

It's one reason why art galleries actually are a good place to hold cocktail parties (we're coming to them, don't worry). As they provide lots of things for mutually aggressive people to look at together rather than facing each other directly.

Both individuals are still highly likely to try to show off to one another about what they know about the artist, of course, but then we're all human.

So, just trust us on this one, because between us we've been at it for over 40 years: a coffee with a view won't taste any different, but your conversation is almost certain to percolate better.

16. More lunched than lunched against

Lunch is coffee-squared. Many of the rules are the same, but it takes longer, costs more and is simply a bigger investment full stop.

But, as ever, we are karmic, we are cool and we know the basics. The Ivy is essentially the same as Wagamama – but we tend to think that if you are paying the bill, the former is unlikely to be strictly necessary.

Let's not get carried away, though. If lunch means a sandwich together in Starbucks (or similar) or a friendly invitation for a bowl of pasta in the office canteen, then we are in "coffee-plus" rather than "coffee-squared" territory.

This chapter is about making the effort to go to a proper restaurant.

Tip 39 – Keep two mobiles strapped in your holsters at all times

If someone has gone to the effort to invite you for lunch, or if you have done them the same courtesy, then they are interested to know a bit more about you than merely ascertaining your views on agenda point three.

Or at least they should be. Lunches are mostly about the Light Side of the Force because most scrappies think they take too long.

But the Dark Side does occasionally go there. We have once or twice been subjected to very hostile lunches by overweening bullies who want to sit you in a corner from which you can't escape, ply you with drink, and get you to spill the beans.

Now we are not big fans of iPhones and strongly suspect that the art of good conversation is now firmly hidden behind the Whatsapp icon. But the fact is that most citizens of Corporationia carry two mobiles.

Well friends, now you're in for a treat. There is only one <u>instruction</u> in this whole book and here it is. Do this right now. Programme the number of your professional iPhone into your private mobile under the reference "1 Chief Exec". The "1" is so that it's the very first contact in your list when you scroll down. Now practice so that you can ring yourself without needing to look at your private phone handset. Now do it again so that it is seamless. Now do it once more and start to enjoy it. Now do it without changing facial expression.

Now you are ready.

All that the disgusting bully will see is a phone call from "Chief Exec" on your iPhone screen. Even if she catches the "1" it won't matter. You are obliged to leave the table and take the call. Even she can't argue with that. Make the phone call last at least twenty minutes (just think, you could be on chapter 18 by then).

Or better still, have your assistant or a colleague at the office (anyone with even an ounce of humanity – i.e. most people you know - will love to do you this "favour", so no stress if you don't have a PA) call her once you are back there to "profoundly apologise" for having had to leave so suddenly. She can surely understand that you had to deal with a crisis at the behest of the top of the office.

Never speak to the bully again. If she had to pay. Don't sweat it. There is only one way to deal with brutal bullies and that is to give it right back to them. Karmically, of course.

Tip 40 – The service matters as much as the food

Back in the civilised world, lunches are indeed for finding out what people are really like. What is their hinterland? What do they like doing? Maybe even a bit about their family and friends. Just ask open questions and let it flow.

The one thing that you want to avoid are irritating interruptions. Any half decent restaurant knows this and if you are a regular then they have every reason to play by the global rules of civilised dining: serve good food and then leave people to enjoy it as they please.

So the one trap you should not fall into if you are doing the inviting is to go to a place that you have never been before. It's like getting your hair cut in a new place for the first time. We all have to do it now and then, but you don't want your boss, or similar, to be present at the act.

In an ideal world, you'll have two or three restaurants that you go to regularly where you know for sure that you'll always get a decent table with friendly service and minimal disturbance.

But if you're just starting out in the lunch game and haven't quite reached nirvana yet, there's no problem, we're just trying to give you a sense of the journey.

Tip 41 – You can probably let them order

We're really hoping that you're not a fussy eater. If you are then you should probably just order a plate of steamed vegetables like you always do. We're not being unsympathetic, it's just that by being fussy you're missing out on so much that's good in life that you are giving a strong hint of being at the outer reaches of our landing zone. There may not be a lot more we can do for you. But we'll still try.

In any case, if you want to take the stress out of choosing, the awkwardness out of going for something expensive, or the potential confrontation out of a cultural mis-step (beef in some parts of India, etc) then just agree with their selection.

If they are paying, then it makes it simpler. If you're in a badly-run restaurant, then you've done everything you can to ensure that the food arrives at the same time. And at some level you have also contrived to compliment their good taste.

Because starting well matters, as we know from chapter 4.

Tip 42 – Courses for horses

Quite often there's just no need to over-complicate things, and so it is with courses. So we'll keep this short and sweet. The simplest way to avoid unnecessary interruptions is for your orders to arrive at the same time. So both have a main course and coffee, or starters and puddings, or a full five-course blow-out (assuming post-prandial productivity is not a concern). Parallelism is the key.

Tip 43 – In vino veritas

We've already discussed how to deal with aggressive attempts to get you to reveal all.

In calmer contexts, sharing alcohol is a further step towards trust-building, and in moderation should not be a problem. If you're being wined and dined by a senior then in most cultures it's for them to suggest alcohol and to choose it. If you're doing the choosing then anyone with even half a brain knows that it's not cool (or karmic) to force drink on people. So just stay within sensible limits and you can't go too far wrong.

We are neither wine buffs nor millionaires, so the issue of selecting some extravagant bottle never arises. But we do know the difference between a Guigal and a Gewurztraminer and don't mind explaining it in the highly unlikely event that you are really, genuinely interested.

But the most likely scenario is that you would simply like to choose something decent that goes well with what you've ordered. If this is becoming a source of tension with your lunch companion, then just call in a mutual friend: most restaurants will be able to recommend something reasonable and you can move swiftly on.

Tip 44 – On bottle grabbers

We are hoping that you are well past the stage of actually wanting to drink more of the bottle than your companion out of greed. There is no karma here. It's also not kosher to (even appear to) ration your colleague's consumption by treating the wine like the Emperor's cookies and squirreling it away where only you can reach it.

Model your wine-bottle management on Yoda's approach to coffee and cookies. Put the bottle in the middle for mutual enjoyment.

Tip 45 – Play Go

We once heard a nice story about a German executive who was invited to play Go with a senior Chinese businessman.

The German had had a few lessons, but was no expert Go strategist. However, he had taken his course with a Chinese teacher in Germany who had told him that in the culture of Go, the way in which one moves the pieces is deemed to be very important. The German had practiced this just as hard as he had practiced the (fiendishly complicated) game itself. As a result of this practice, he was, by Chinese standards, mediocre both at playing the game and at moving the pieces.

Now it's apparently not that hard to get to a reasonable level at Go by playing on the internet. But by the standards of a typical foreigner, the German had developed outstanding Go technique from a body language point of view. The German, of course, lost the match, but he won the contract because he had managed to convey a sense of respect for another's culture.

Taking a meal together must surely be the oldest trust-building ritual in all of human evolution. If you think even half as much about how you eat as you do about what you eat, you won't go far wrong.

17. On cocktails, receptions, lifts and coffee queues

Cocktails and receptions look like intimidating minefields. They seem to offer such enormous scope to offend, embarrass, mis-speak and generally cock it up that surely you should never go to them. Add in the noise, the lights, the possibility for fashion *faux pas* and the karmic advice must unquestionably be to keep well clear. Right?

We disagree. More or less.

Tip 46 – Two a month, tops

For the fact is that cocktails and receptions are a great chance to meet a huge number of people rapidly, without having to hang around if they are tedious or to stay until coffee is served as a minimum.

One of the few simple rules to follow is not to go to too many. Mainly because this just looks a bit sad. But also because familiarity breeds contempt and might lead you to start drinking too much. At which point cocktails go from being a great opportunity to find a few Sanghistas, to the perfect opportunity to make yourself look like a complete fool.

Tip 47 – Two a night, tops

You will therefore have to learn how to ration your alcohol intake when people keep coming around to re-fill your glass. The easiest way is to start with an orange juice.

This has two main benefits. First, it means you won't actually be thirsty when you have your first glass of champagne. Second, it will help you to keep a clear head during the second-most dangerous part of the evening: the first half-hour.

Tip 48 – Wait two quarters, and you've cracked it

The first half-hour (which actually starts from the time at which 15 to 20 people turn up) is the ceremonial phase of the evening. Seniors talk to seniors and the middle-ranks and juniors must shuffle their feet and make do with one another's company without being too raucous.

If you want to use a cocktail event to pass on a good idea to the CEO, NEVER try to do it in the first half hour. At this point, she must work the room, say hello to everyone, especially the important people, and generally be active. Even if you should find that she walks over to you, it will only be so that she looks busy for a moment, so don't blurt early and muck it all up.

After this showing-off phase is over, most people relax and loosen up a bit (the second glass of champagne – for them – is probably helping) and you will be much freer to speak to whomever you want to seek out. More importantly, they will have "said hello" to all of the people that they had to be nice to and hence they may have a bit of time to listen.

Tip 49 – Stand in doorways and leave before the witching hour

We appreciate that this sounds like something out of Harry Potter, but it's actually good advice. Much easier than walking over to the chiefs is to let them come to you. It's not actually that hard. Hint: apart from in children's fantasy literature, people cannot in fact walk through walls.

Add to this the fact that any senior colleagues with social skills will need to move around the "cocktail space" (they nearly always have inter-connecting doors and archways as a minimum – you can usefully spend the first 30 minutes doing a bit of reconnaissance) and you will find that over time they come to you. Simple.

The final point is just tip 44 all over again and it's one of the best things about cocktails and receptions. <u>There are no rules about when you should leave</u>. The only rule that we would add is that it's not cool to (be seen) hang(ing) around at the end. Just add excess alcohol and this – the witching hour – suddenly becomes, by far, <u>the</u> most dangerous section of the whole event.

So once you've met two or three interesting people (any more than that would be a world record in one evening) just give yourself a ring on your iPhone, make your excuses and go home and watch a bit of Ray Mears.

Post-script: it's always well-seen to walk over to the host as you are leaving and simply to say "thank you for the invitation". It never even occurs to many people.

Tip 50 – A deviation on lifts and coffee queues

There is a great episode of "Yes, Prime Minister" in which Sir Humphrey is unable to repress his sheer delight at an upcoming State funeral.

"Rather distasteful, Humphrey" mutters PM Jim Hacker.

"Not at all, half the world's leaders will be there and you won't have to travel any distance at all to meet them. Just think of the saving to the Treasury".

As ever, Humphrey is cynical, but with reason. For the fact is that the opportunities for "brief, but rich" diplomatic activity afforded by such events is indeed truly remarkable. "Brush pasts" is the technical term.

Now without wishing to be macabre or overly insensitive, there are two locations in your current working environment (assuming you are not a full-time tele-worker) that display all of the diplomatic advantages of a State funeral.

They are generally known as the lift and the coffee queue.

Now here we are operating in a booby-trapped part of the jungle. If one-liners aren't your thing or you find it hard to remember names and faces, there is no shame in hunting elsewhere.

We will simply close this chapter with the observation that lifts and coffee queues share many similarities with cocktails and receptions, but without the need to sacrifice an evening or (for our female readership, in the main) to get your hair done. But you will need to be deft in your handling of the situation as you will be operating outside of the boundaries of standard social protocol.

We'll leave it to you to figure out what we mean, but with one final word of warning. It is in no way karmic to get a reputation for hanging around in lifts and doorways…

18. Whose dinner party is it anyway?

We know what you're thinking, because in the last few chapters he's almost disappeared. Minimal tail-wagging. Barely a "let me at 'em" to be seen. Quite frankly, you've almost started to miss him. What's happened? Has Scrappy given up the ghost? Has he admitted defeat and retired to the Cotswolds to write his memoirs?

Not a bit of it. For once he's put his thinking cap on. Because you have succeeded in riling him. You can hide in plain sight for a while, quite a long while usually, but eventually he will notice.

And now he's going to fight back. Because that's what Scrappies do. It's the only way they know.

Yes, you've guessed it. You're about to receive an invitation to a dinner party.

Tip 51 – Afghan shouting rituals

Dinner parties are almost always awful for karmic types and Scrappy knows it. Apart from in the rarest of cases, put 8 to 10 people with some professional connections around the same table and what you've actually created is a para-meeting.

Bring a few spouses along and you may (if we're following Debrett's for a brief moment, which indeed you should) be able to delay the real work talk until after coffee.

But in all cases, barring those so karmically rare that we are not sure they have ever actually existed beyond the realms of theory, what you rapidly end up with is a ritual showing-off forum.

And ritual showing-off is boring. Unless you are a boring boor. And that is why scrappies, unbelievable as it may seem, actually like DPs.

One of us used to have a friend who had spent a fair amount of time in Afghanistan. He explained that a common ritual in that part of the world before two (it's always) men will sit down and talk to each other in a calm and reasonable manner about business is that each will basically shout and yell directly into one another's faces for a good ten to fifteen minutes.

This is tiring for all concerned, and it's not clear that anyone really enjoys it. But it has evolved as a way of credibly signalling that you are sufficiently interested to talk to your "opponent" that you are willing to endure a quarter of an hour of loud and unpleasant noise.

We are not sure that the modern dinner party is directly Afghan-inspired. But the thought has occurred to us.

We manage to dodge most dinner party invitations but we don't always succeed, and whenever we do go along to one, even the most considerate hosts never manage consistently to divert the conversation away from the usual bragging topics of:

(a) who has recently been on holiday to the farthest-flung destination (amount of pleasure derived irrelevant);

(b) who has been over-charged the most for essential domestic repairs in recent weeks (the basics of good negotiation irrelevant – it's a salary competition by proxy);

(c) whose children's school fees are the most outrageous (we refer the honourable gentleman to the reply we gave some moments ago).

What is worse, at some point the "host" will invariably "call the dinner to order" and ask the invited congregation to debate the merits of some burning topic of the day. (See the chapter 11).

The best that we can say is that this is another area where greater karmic research is needed. Perhaps there do exist corners of the world in which professional colleagues meet on a Saturday evening in groups of 8 – 10, possibly including the WAGs (or BAHs, as the case may be), over a meal and actually enjoy a thoughtful conversation.

N.B. WAGs: wives and girlfriends, BAHs: boyfriends and husbands.

If so, please write to us and tell us how you do it and we'll be sure to give you a mention in the 2nd edition.

Tip 52 – Find an(y) other way

This is the best we can do on dinner parties. We have given you ways to handle coffees, lunches, drinks, receptions, lifts and queues. But the seventh day is, or at least should be, for rest and reflection.

Subject to greater wisdom being sent to us from corporate co-travellers elsewhere in the galaxy, we just hope you don't work in a world in which dinner parties are viewed as an essential ingredient for corporate participation, progress and promotion.

For surely there has to be a better way.

Futuristic Karmic Jazz

19. I don't want to change the world

Well at least that's what Billy Bragg claimed in his famous song. But he was, in fact, looking for a "New England" (as well as another girl), as he has since made clear.

Now Billy is just the kind of person that you _would_ want to sit next to at a dinner party. He's interesting. He's read books. And if he gets on his high horse (which he is surely far too polite to do), then you could vaguely glance in the direction of a guitar you've hidden behind the sofa (but not very well) and he's capable of setting it all to music and cheering everyone up with a tune.

Politically, he has a radical agenda, as he is fully entitled to do.

We don't.

For a start, it just wouldn't be credible. As you know by now, between us we have worked for over 40 years in some very large organisations.

As a result we have met corporate people from all over the world for meetings, coffees, lunches and more. And our considered view is that they are about as good, and bad, as all of the other people that we have come across from other walks of life: from government officials to social workers, charitable volunteers to CEOs.

Tip 53 – It's the context that matters (yes, again)

Sorry to keep banging on about this context thing, but in our experience it's crucial.

Sensible people have known throughout human history that any group or organisation that involves human beings cooperating together can go bad if you regularly let them get: tired, hungry, or even just collectively reasonably irritable on a regular basis.

And if you forget to keep an eye on the chicken coop, then the foxes will come and eat them. Truly bad people exist in all walks of life, but most people aren't really bad, they're simply too easily tempted.

Just ask anyone in the advertising business.

And that's why human societies have developed everything from tribal elders, sacred texts, constitutions and – yes – even annual accounts, all with varying degrees of success at providing a context that keeps most of the people on the straight and narrow most of the time.

Because, frankly, that's probably enough.

Keynes famously thought that in the future it would only be necessary for people to work about three hours per day.

Now he was a pretty civilised chap, albeit with some interestingly outré proclivities, such that he may just have neglected to reflect on quite how much trouble an unsupervised bunch of scrappies could cause if given a regular supply of twenty-one free hours per day and sufficient regular income to satisfy their basic needs.

For as we have seen in chapter 13, in the long-run it's important to think these things through.

The irony is that these days the boot is rather on the other foot.

Tip 54 – The squeeze is on, we've got to face it

By which we mean that life is getting harder for people like us who want to combine a career and a life.

Keynes was flat wrong about increased leisure time, at least for the denizens of modern-day Corporationia. Most people nowadays have to work harder, for longer, and then have to keep an eye on the Blackberry in the evening when any civilised family should be sitting down and eating a meal together.

We're happy with a very broad definition indeed of what civilisation means, by the way.

But civilisation matters, because it's better than the alternative. Not all anarchists are teenagers, but emotionally, they are barely even that.

To put it another way, you don't have to spend your whole, or even hardly any, of your life going to art galleries, museums, concerts and the theatre. But virtually anyone with anything about them whatsoever would be willing to admit, in private, to the closest member of their Sangha, that they have benefited personally from even a small dose of access to what old-farts would call "culture". N.B. as we've said, we are broad-minded, but we do draw the line at that Benny Hill Youtube retrospective, nevertheless.

Tip 55 – Calm down, guys

Ok. Rant over.

It's just that from a karmic point of view western (read corporate) society does seem to us to be missing at least one important trick…

Thanks to modern medical research and technology, we are all living longer. And karmic psychologists (start with the Kahneman book in the annex, if you're a doubter) are having more and more success pointing out that for "knowledge workers" at the very least, full retirement may not be all it's cracked up to be.

We don't know about you, but sixty or even sixty-five doesn't actually feel that old any more. And the prospect of twenty-five to thirty years at the end of one's life without any work to do at all seems quite frightening. Plus the numbers clearly aren't going to add up for society to keep paying for all of these shades of ever greyer hair.

At least not without a lot more babies and/ or migrants, but these big issues are way off the reservation for this book. Maybe some other time.

Returning to the matter at hand, Gaia is duly getting on the case and as a result we see more and more people in their sixties and seventies working "some of the time" in all sorts of "low-impact" jobs (yes, like corporate paper pushing). By which we mean "low-impact" in a physical sense, of course. We have our egos too you know.

So far, so karmic.

The bigger puzzle is what's going on in "30 to 50 or so" age-bracket. And the simple answer is: way, way too much.

In many important respects, Western (corporate) society has clearly moved on from the "Mad Men" world of the 1950s, in which men wore the trousers, women bent over, and divorce rates were miraculously low. And we are all much the better for it.

Tip 56 – Get established, then slow down if you need to

But our feeling is that we have yet to make the karmic leap to "slowing down once established" that a combination of common sense and longer life expectancy implies. This is getting conceptual, so it may be time for another picture.

Simple picture number 3 – the Karmic Curve

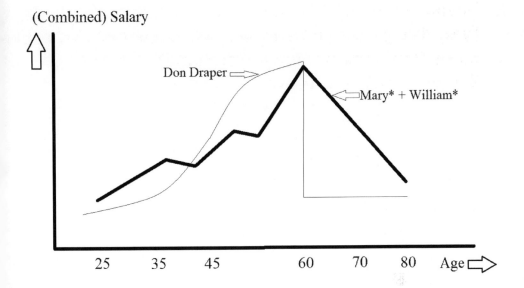

(Combined) Salary

Don Draper

Mary* + William*

25 35 45 60 70 80 Age

Abstract for a moment from the fact that – if you take this chart too literally - we will earn the same combined, inflation-adjusted salary as Don Draper (the star of the hit TV series Mad Men) aged 60. Regrettably, the top ad men earn a lot more than we do in real-life. But we can dream! Can't we?

Also, please don't read too much into the steadily downwards trend post-60. That just means more jacuzzi time during our 30-, then 20-, then 10-hour working weeks as we mature gracefully. All Don has is his measly pension!

And give us a little break at least: we're just trying to illustrate a more pleasant vision of the future, not defend a PhD in applied statistics…

The real point is that the implicit career-age-promotion-dynamics of early 21st century corporate Scrappy-world are all wrong. They still correspond to the world of 1950s New York advertising when nowadays we have (almost) all stopped smoking, the three-martini lunch is unheard of, and it's "trendy" to wear a Fitbit (or so we are given to believe).

And we all know who is to blame: step forward Scrappy-Doo and his indomitable friends. They just can't wait, can they?

Tip 57 – We are not alone

But we are not the only pioneers bravely (wo)manning this frosty outpost. A really very clever person, quite possibly of the Maynard Keynes variety, called Anne-Marie Slaughter has recently written a book called "Unfinished Business" that tries to open this particular can of worms with (just a bit more!) academic rigour.

Professor Slaughter, a major source of inspiration for this book, is also famous for having stepped down from a very high-profile job at the US State Department to spend more time with her family at a moment when that was just what they needed. Kudos.

Simple picture number 3 is our humble contribution to further stirring the debate that she is more than capably kicking off.

AMS has gotten some stick from hard-core feminists for having the temerity to suggest that women can't have it all.

We just think she deserves some credit for stating the blindingly obvious to anyone in their 30s and 40s who has ever actually tried to manage a career (make that two), a marriage, several children, and a waistline/ weekend season ticket at your football club (delete as appropriate), all at the same time.

You can't. It's not possible.

A cleverer critique would be to say that AMS has simply pointed out that you can't have it all, <u>all at the same time</u>. So some things will just have to wait. And given that children (like scrappies – funny that) are not very good at patience, maybe it's the day job that will have to give. For now.

To try to be a bit more scientific about <u>when</u> you're likely to have to start slowing down temporarily, we reckon that it's the roughly 6 or so years from when you get pregnant with your <u>second</u> child(ren) until the youngest is around 5. Plus some of the 5-7 years when your kids are passing through adolescence (we can't wait…).

Probably, that is. Life is just not that predictable. But these are the best guesses that we've been able to collect from within our Sangha.

So in case we haven't been clear enough, our "line with two kinks" labelled "Mary* + William*" demonstrates the kind of earnings profile that talented couples (who are somehow able, between them, to find ways of slowing down at those times when the domestic pressure is really on) <u>should</u> be able to achieve, if only we lived in a saner corporate jungle.

If we were better at drawing, we'd call it the Karmic Curve.

20. The Jungle VIP

We have stressed throughout this book that we are not really interested in becoming the King of the Swingers. But Jungle VIP does have a certain ring to it, nonetheless.

We have also been lucky enough between us to have met, and in some cases even worked directly with, a handful of truly extraordinary leaders. We are not going to name them as their egos are already plenty big enough as it is: an essential part of the package.

But our principal observation is that most of what got them to where they are could not be taught. It probably could not be taught out of them either.

To paraphrase a little, John Maynard Keynes had a truly phenomenal brain. And Donald Trump has a truly phenomenal ego. Trying to replicate the first is a matter for neuro-science. It's simply not our field.

Now it's just possible that you could try to model your own ego on that of Donald Trump, but why on earth would you want to?

Odious manners and flagrant insecurity are simply not part of our leadership paradigm.

For many of these <u>extraordinary</u> leaders, most of what drives them on and on, and on, is some combination of the instinctive and the intuitive. They would never read through a book like this, for example, because they wouldn't really be that interested.

What manifests itself as "leadership" in their case is more akin to the answer to a deep, personal psychological need rather than any actively thought-through life strategy.

But please notice that we have used the word extraordinary very deliberately. Extraordinary is nowadays often taken to mean excellent. But that isn't its original or purer meaning. *Extra*-ordinary simply means out of the ordinary. Or highly unusual, to put it another way.

We are less interested in being extraordinary and more interested in being karmic. By which – as we have tried to show throughout this book - we mean having regular recourse to very simple things like thinking, listening and slowing matters down to a speed that the limited human brain can comprehend.

It's not rocket science, but many people find it deeply threatening. Because it does question whether they should be mindlessly chasing the next short-term ego boost, before immediately turning to hunt down the next one, and the next one after that.

Tip 58 – It's *The Republic,* captain, but not as we know it

Plato's *The Republic* contains the idea that men (this was circa 380 B.C. remember) should seek public office not out of greed or ambition, but because they have come to realise that they are less-badly-fitted for its burdens than their peers.

It's a beautiful notion, but today we have Youtube. We are all fallible. And everyone knows it.

Ultimately, if you are determined to climb the greasy pole as fast as possible and at all costs, then neither we, nor even Plato, are going to come anywhere close to stopping you.

You are almost certainly driven by impulses beyond your own control. And even if could observe and internalise the attendant costs (because there will be costs – modern corporate and government leadership is just too frenetic) to your family, your health and your sanity, that would be unlikely to have any dissuasive impact either.

But for anyone and everyone else - who has plenty of drive, but who is also capable of flicking <u>off</u> the turbo switch from time to time – and who has been indulgent enough to join us on this journey, we hope, at the very least, that we have given you a few ideas about how things could be just a little bit different in the future.

21. Conclusion

For we are not seeking a revolution. And we don't want to smash the system.

But we've got that song "The King of the Swingers" from the Jungle Book in our ears … and it's not unconstitutional to have a dream … on either side of the Atlantic.

So, if fairy tales can still come true … if you're among the young at heart …

Then all we are saying is – c'mon corporate titans – just give us a little swing from the current 120 beats per minute of Scrappy-world techno, to the smoother rhythms of futuristic corporate Karmic Jazz.

It can be all the rage at Davos next year, if you only want it to be.

'Cos Barack and Michelle are gonna need something to dance to, after all.

So take it away fellas. It's over to you.

Epilogue

There is a beautiful and optimistic idea in the more progressive strands of Jewish thinking that, embedded within the sometimes unhealthy obsession with writing everything down and codifying knowledge in books, comes the possibility that future generations may come to understand more than their forebears.

In this sense, whilst all truly holy texts and scriptures deserve to be treated with respect and reverence, it is not irreverent at least to consider the possibility that the sum of human wisdom may, given a following wind, increase down the ages.

We got this idea from a close friend of ours whose father died not so long ago. His father was a Jewish man from a "mixed" Viennese marriage between his father's Ashkenazy mother and Catholic father. Our friend's father sometimes struggled to reconcile all of this, born as he was in England just after the Second World War. And although he was secular in all formal respects, he had within him a quiet, maybe even sub-conscious, impulse to pass on thoughts and ideas – old-world wisdom, in fact – when he could.

But our friend's father was a man who preferred art and music to words and so the thoughts and ideas often came in semiotic form.

Our friend has tried to explain this system to us, if system is the right word. And the best way we can understand it is as a method of coding messages to be handed down through the ages.

We put this part at the end in case you might think we were on some sort of mystical mission. We are not and we don't think our friend is either.

But we were touched by a short story our friend told us and so we tell it to you as our epilogue.

A few years before our friend's father died, our friend got married. Now he himself was not Jewish, as his father had married a British woman with an Anglican English mother and a Protestant Scottish father. He had never faced the slightest pressure to marry a Jewish girl. Why would he?

And indeed as it turned out he married a mainly secular Catholic girl and they are now one of the happiest couples we know.

And our friend's father seemed pleased for his son and never said or hinted any different. Then, one day, a propos nothing and without explanation, our friend's father sent him a web-link to a BBC Radio 4 recording of a "Prom" concert of the Mahler IV.

The accompanying message simply said that it was one of the most beautiful recordings that our friend's father had ever heard.

The son was a man of books, art and music in more or less that order. So he listened to the concert, but he also read about Gustav Mahler and how he had achieved some prominence and even acceptance in 19th-century Viennese society by marrying a Catholic woman and, at the very least, not displaying his Jewishness openly.

By allowing the music to speak for him, in other words.

And so it was that some time after his father's untimely death several years later, the son, our friend, came to realise that although his father had never said very much to him directly about the marriage, he had blessed it fully in his own coded, and maybe even purely subconscious, way.

At least that is what our friend thinks was the particular piece of wisdom handed down to him across the ages.

And now our friend has three children himself and he tells us that he has this deeply encoded notion somewhere, perhaps purely in his subconscious, that one day they might enjoy reading this book.

Possibly even with the Mahler IV playing in the background.

Bibliography

Books/ articles directly referenced

- Blink, Malcolm Gladwell

- Debrett's New Guide to Etiquette and Modern Manners, John Morgan

- Financial Times articles *passim* by Lucy Kellaway

- On death and dying, Elisabeth Kübler-Ross

- Quiet, Susan Cain

- Thinking Fast and Slow, Daniel Kahneman

- Unfinished Business: Women Men Work Family, Anne-Marie Slaughter

Further reading/ books that influenced us

- Getting to Yes, Roger Fisher and William L. Ury

- Happiness, Richard Layard

- Meditations, Marcus Aurelius

- Obliquity, John Kay
- Tender is the Night, F. Scott Fitzgerald
- The Art of Power, Thich Nhat Hanh
- The Economic Consequences of Peace, John Maynard Keynes
- The First Ten Books, Confucius
- The Republic, Plato
- The Righteous Mind, Jonathan Haidt

Keeping in touch

We are always keen to learn, so if you would have (constructive, if we may) feedback on the book, or ideas about the topics we raise, please feel free to email us at:

karmicideas@hotmail.com

You can also take a look at our website:

www.karmic-curve.com

And follow us on Twitter:

@MIWilliamauthor

Printed in Great Britain
by Amazon